5 Easy Steps to a Happy Birthday!
A practical, funny guide to a
Happy Birthday every single year!

© 2020 by Michèle Olson. All rights reserved.
Published by Lake Girl Publishing
Green Bay, WI
www.LakeGirlPublishing.com
info@LakeGirlPublishing.com
Copyright © year 2020
All rights reserved

ISBN: 978-1-7343628-3-1

Table of Contents

Why this book	4
Birthday Step One	8
Birthday Step Two	13
Birthday Step Three	19
Birthday Step Four	28
Birthday Step Five	35
Introverted Birthday	45
Extroverted Birthday	48
Expensive Birthday	51
Low-Budget Birthday	54
20 All-Over-the-Place Tips	57
10 Ideas for Celebrations	63
A Song and Wish for You	67
Other Books by Michèle	68
Meet the Author	71

Why This Book?

Wondering why this book exists? I'm glad you asked!

Somewhere in my mid 30's, after a crappy birthday, I had an epiphany. It's up to me to have a happy birthday. After speaking to many people, it's become apparently clear. Not only do a vast majority not experience a happy birthday, but they don't know how to have a happy birthday! That's a national travesty! A birthday is special. It is your one unique day when you made a grand arrival on the planet and told the world you were here. It should be celebrated, and I don't mean with a convenience store cupcake plopped on your desk accompanied by an off-key rendition of the tune we all know.

This book is not for kids, because their happy birthdays are up to their parents. (If you are a parent and not providing a happy birthday for your child, you should still read this. It will spur some ideas for you.) This book is for adults... whether you used to have happy birthdays and now you don't...whether you think you don't care if you have a happy birthday (I'm calling you out — you do), or whether happy birthdays have eluded you, this book is for you. From now on, if you follow this book, you will have an incredibly happy birthday.

No better than that— a HAPPY BIRTHDAY!!!

In fact, you'll put a big star on the calendar and wait with high anticipation for 364 days for your SPECIAL DAY! Ready to love your birthday and make it happy? No, I mean REALLY HAPPY? Let's go!

Acknowledgements:

To Patty, my friend who already knows how to celebrate!

I praise you because I am fearfully and wonderfully made; your works are wonderful, I know that full well.

Psalm 139:14, New International Version

1
Birthday Step Number One: *Never Work on Your Birthday*

Birthday Step Number One: Never Work on Your Birthday

It's no coincidence that this is step number one. Right up front, you have to do this step right. There's no leeway. I've heard people say they like to work on their birthday because they want to be with the people they know. You can be with them every other working day of the year, but this is not the day. If they are the acknowledging type, they will acknowledge you the day before or the day after your big day. If you have really close work friends, invite them to take a day off and participate in your birthday plan. (More coming on that!)

So, let me repeat the all-important first step of birthday happiness.

Never Work on Your Birthday.

Here's why. You don't have time in your special day to allot eight or more hours to your usual routine. No way, no how. Now, what if you are an emergency brain surgeon and it happens to be your birthday. Let's say someone hunts you down and demands only you can save their life if you operate on their brain. Do you think this dire situation means you should stray from step number one?

NO! Time to memorize this step.

Never Work on Your Birthday.

If you don't follow this step, you may have an okay birthday once in a while. Passable. Yawn. But overall, when you look back over most of them, you will be disappointed. And, aren't you tired of being disappointed?

So, what's the number one step you must follow to have a happy birthday?

_____.

Fill this in and sign below.

I agree and promise that I will not work on my birthday.

X _____.

2
Birthday Step Number Two: *Take Control of Your Day*

Birthday Step Number Two: Take Control of Your Day

Now that you've followed birthday step number one, birthday step number two should be much easier. Your employer (should you have one) is not expecting you at work. If you have a regular volunteer schedule, step number one also counts. Don't schedule any work/volunteer/giving of your time or anything similar on your day. (This is an excellent time to go back and review step number one if you still find it confusing in any way.)

If, in the past you have

celebrated your birthday with activities planned by others that didn't tickle you pink and send you into endless giggles of glee —then put the kibosh on anything you get wind of that may be happening surrounding your birthday. There's a highly recommended method of stopping things from happening that you aren't thrilled about. It's two little letters: NO! Or, if you're the polite sort — "No, Thank you." Don't fall for anything that smacks of a surprise party if that's not your thing. If it is, embrace it and enjoy, but only if you love the idea.

Back to taking control of your

day. Forget about anything that you should be doing or has been forced upon you. You have been given a magical day to do whatever you want! (As long as it's moral and legal.)

Take some time to think about what you want to do. There will be suggestions and tips as this book progresses, but I don't want to put any thoughts in your head just yet. This is a time for some free form thinking on your part. There are no rules when it comes to dreaming about your day. It will help to get a bit frivolous and goofy as you think about all the possibilities a day holds when those 24 hours lie ahead

just for you to do what you like.
At this point in the process,
don't give yourself limits like
money. Don't pre-judge ideas.
Simply take the time to dream.

Set aside at least an hour on
your half birthday to dream
about your real birthday.
Consider taking off a half day
(If you have a scheduled job)
just to plan your real birthday.
See? This just keeps getting
better and better!

So, what's step number two, to have a happy birthday?

_____.

Fill this in and sign below.

I agree to take control of the day for my next birthday.

X _____.

3
Birthday Step Number Three: *You Must Have a Plan*

Birthday Step Number Three: You Must Have a Plan

Who was it that said "If you fail to plan, you plan to fail?" The magic box attributes the quote to Benjamin Franklin. But then, wasn't he the same guy out flying kites in storms? Was that a good plan? Hmmm. Still, he was on to something.

As wondrous as a birthday can be, you can't just sit on your chair and wait for fairy Godmothers to show up with bluebirds to fix you some lovely attire. Besides, no one knows more about what trips your trigger than you!

Do you need a plan A and a plan B? Not a bad idea, especially if plan A is weather related. Or, if you're working on your birthday, everything will have to take place after work. Wait, WHAT???? Stop what you're doing and go back to Step One. Do not pass Go, do not collect a Happy Birthday!

This is a good place for a disclaimer. If you only follow part of the birthday advice in this book, well, it's a free country and you can do whatever you want. HOWEVER, do not expect to claim the best birthday possible if you are fudging on the steps. Don't be one of those step-skippers roaming around seeing what steps they can skip. Follow each step and experience a happy birthday—barring hurricanes, locusts, and food poisoning. As far as you have control —stick to the steps. Now, let's get back to those.

What makes a plan a plan and not just a thought? That happens when you write it down. Writing it down has its own special ability to clarify your thinking and keep you on track. When you write it down, you can come back to it several days later and determine if you have lost your mind with what you produced, or if you think it's possibly the most brilliant thing you've ever thought. Or, you might land somewhere in the middle. It's all good.

Maybe you are trying to be tricky, and you want a birthday with no plan. I see what you did there. You want a day with nothing ahead of you. But, here's the thing. You have to plan to not have a plan. That's still a plan. Keep thinking. It will all make sense!

If you need help with some plans, there are plenty of suggestions ahead. Use them as springboards to ideas you love. There are so many possibilities! But, don't plan yet. Get through the overview of the steps first.

(Boy, I can be bossy, right? It's for your own good, I promise!)

Here's another important point – don't count on anyone else to make your birthday happy! This is such a critical statement that it should almost be a step unto itself, but five steps work, so we'll stick with that. Here's the deal – if you wait for others to make your birthday happy, it won't work. You are large and in charge of your own birthday! Now, if others contribute in the way of gifts, dinners, and parties etc. — all because you wanted these things — think of them as icing on the cake. They are nice sidebars you can be accept with gratitude. But they are not the cake. You are in charge of the cake. (Using cake as a metaphor here, keep up!)

But speaking of cake! Get some literal cake that day, if you love cake. And for Pete's sake don't get a marble cake! I don't believe it's really anyone's favorite. Marble cake pleases no one. The vanilla lovers are disappointed, and the chocolate lovers are bummed. Choose a real cake—not a wishy-washy marble cake! This is a celebration people, not a compromise!

Getting your cake or pie or donut or vegetable tray should all be part of your plan for your day. This is a day to eat what you love! There are no calories on your birthday! I'm sure of it! If you choose a healthy eating style most of the year, you can have what you want on your birthday. It's YOUR day, remember?

So, what's step number three for having a happy birthday?

_____.

Fill this in and sign below.

I agree to have a plan for my next birthday.

X _____.

4
Birthday Step Number Four: *Be Intentional About Absolute Enjoyment*

Birthday Step Number Four: Be Intentional About Absolute Enjoyment

I wish we could live every day as if it's our birthday, because we'd be a crazily, happy bunch of people walking around. That's not feasible, or reasonable, but we can surely make it a must for this one day. You have to work on your brain before your birthday, so you have the right attitude. If you are a person who is easily frustrated or bothered because things didn't go as you planned, you must conquer this step. Short of zombies taking over the town and doing away with everyone, you must determine with all that is within you — this day will be the best day of the year for you. Nothing can mar it, spoil it, wreck it, hamper it, or derail how you will enjoy the day. Train your brain for this truth.

Does that mean you might have to be flexible with some of your plans? It may, but that's where your determined intentionality will ensure that this day will be fantastic! Say you planned to go to a movie you've been waiting to come out and suddenly the movie theater gets infested with frogs! (It could happen.) This should not wreck your day. You simply move onto another one of your ideas from your plan. Lucky you if you had frog catching in your birthday plan! See, it's your day, and you can do a million different things. Be intentional. No matter what gets in the way of a plan, it won't matter. You will be having a happy birthday by adjusting to the disrupting circumstance and moving in a different direction.

If you allow your feathers to get ruffled and feel as though you were robbed of something — you'll put a damper on the day. Not allowed. You are having an intentional day of joy and happiness. No circumstance can goof it up. Magic days like your birthday morph themselves into something special even if a beginning plan doesn't work. That's what they do. If you, by chance don't get that, or see that as possibility — there's your next thinking assignment. A happy birthday is there and possible. You must be flexible if a hiccup occurs. It shouldn't diminish the enjoyment of your day. If you have a personality bent on fretting, your birthday is the one day you can let that go.

You can go back to being a curmudgeon the other 364 days a year, but it won't work for the happy birthday plan. Besides, getting a new 'tude on this one day may be a catalyst for turning that frown into a smile on many other days. You might find out it's an easier way to live…or not. Curmudgeon away if that's your thing — just not on your birthday when it comes to deviating from your plans.

The one exception? If you really feel being a crabby person would make you happy on your birthday, I have to give you this one. Feel free to sit on the porch, yell at the neighbor kids, and complain about the government.

So, what's step number four when it comes to having a happy birthday?

_____.

Fill this in and sign below.

I agree to be intentional about absolute enjoyment.

X _____.

5
Birthday Step Number Five: *Own Your Birthday Conversation*

Birthday Step Number Five: Own Your Birthday Conversation

Anticipating a fun birthday is part of the fun of having a birthday! Read that again. To all those people who tell me their birthday is not a big deal and they don't celebrate much anymore, or birthdays are for kids I say: WRONG! You were born knowing that the day you landed on the planet was for you, a special day. Circumstances, family environments, or disappointments may have made it safer for you to retreat from celebrating. If you look deep inside, you'll find a little flickering flame that doesn't want to be sad, or let down, or give up on birthdays. Building up a wall against birthdays because you have had crummy days is normal. Now you have this book to change that around! Don't fret about all the birthdays you have possibly wasted so far. Nothing can be done about that. However, do own your birthday conversation from now on!

What does that mean in a tangible way?

First, assess the voice in your head, your self-talk. Start to speak positively about your birthday to yourself. Get excited about what a great day it can be if you follow the rules. Put a big red circle around the day on your calendar. Do a ten, nine, eight, countdown before it gets here. Tell yourself what a great day it's going to be, because it will be a fantastic day!

Next, there are the words you speak to others. Let's look at a possible conversation.

Person in your life: "Hey, seems like someone is having a birthday next week! How do you feel about that?"

You: "Excited! My birthday is going to be awesome. I've planned a spectacular day doing things I love."

Person in your life: "Don't you have to work that day?"

You: "Are you kidding?? I will never work on my birthday again, since I read this great book on how to have a happy birthday. You should get a copy!"

Ha! Of course, you can come up with a better conversation, but catch the enthusiasm of knowing ahead of time that you will have a fantastic birthday. Own the words you say about your birthday in your head and to other people. It's part of the fun—the anticipation and joy that surrounds a happy birthday every year spills into your everyday life. You wait and see, it will happen!

So, what's step number five when it comes to having a happy birthday?

_____.

Fill this in and sign below.

I agree to own my birthday conversation.

X _____.

Quick Review:

Birthday Step Number One:
Never Work on Your Birthday

Birthday Step Number Two:
Take Control of Your Day

Birthday Step Number Three:
You Must Have a Plan

Birthday Step Number Four:
Be Intentional About Absolute Enjoyment

Birthday Step Number Five:
Own Your Birthday Conversation

That was pretty fun, right?

So, there you have it! The Five Steps, all here for you to change up how you celebrate your birthday. Implement them all and you are well on your way to splendid, happy birthdays for the rest of your life. Once people start seeing you have a wonderful birthday, they may ask how it came about. You can try to explain it, or you can get them their own copy of this book. Remember, yours is used because you filled in each section and signed your name. (You did sign each section, right? Don't forget! Writing it down and signing your name will help seal the deal with yourself!)

But, wait! There's more!

Take a look at some distinct birthday suggestions for personality traits and consider the crazy suggestions of what's possible.

5 Tips for an Introverted Birthday

1) Travel somewhere so you can be away from people who might "overbirthday" you in a way you don't like. Or imply you are gone, but stay home with the curtains closed.

2) Do things that you don't get to do but are easy to do alone. Movies would be a good option, or binge watch something you've been waiting to see. You might like to spend the whole day reading and eating snacks.

3) Order in food and set up a buffet for one or have dinner with one or two people. Aim for dining with your very favorite

people.

4) Take a tour. You can enjoy the day, but no one will know it's your birthday.

5) Take a lesson. Have you always wanted to take a flying lesson, painting class, or make your own pottery? Go do the thing you've always wanted to do. The beauty of being an introvert is you don't have to worry about anyone else's availability.

Add your own ideas:

5 Tips for an Extroverted Birthday

1) Throw yourself a BIG party. Make it a fun theme that you love. Go all out!

2) Go on a trip with tons of your friends. You pick the destination and itinerary, it's your birthday.

3) Take a cooking class or any class with a bunch of friends. End the night with your favorite cake and the place of your choosing.

4) Karaoke! You know you want to perform. It's your birthday! You can own the stage.

5) Movies! Plays! Concerts!

Festivals! Amusement Parks! Go, Go, Go!

Add your own ideas:

5 Tips for an Expensive Birthday

1) Rent a plane and take people somewhere unexpected.

2) Go around handing out money, randomly, as you see fit to anyone you want.

3) Rent out an entire restaurant, theatre, or bowling alley. Fill it with people or keep it for yourself and a few close friends.

4) Deliver your favorite cake or something yummy to a place in your town—enough for everyone. Suggestions? Senior living homes, homeless shelters, police and fire stations—you get the picture.

5) Buy tons of copies of this book and give one to everyone you know. Tell them, "I'm having a happy birthday today and I want to make sure you have one on your birthday, too!"

Add your own ideas:

5 Tips for a Low-Budget Birthday

1) Go to the library and take out a book you've been dying to read. Go to a favorite spot and read it while sipping your favorite beverage. No rushing, no schedule!

2) Get a stack of 1-dollar bills and walk around handing them out to people.

3) Meander all day around your town and stop at places you've never been. Or go to a close-by town and explore.

4) Check out local museums, art galleries, parks...someplace new. Try a new restaurant or café.

5) Buy a few copies of this book and give one to your close circle of friends. Tell them, "I'm having a happy birthday today and I want to make sure you have one, too!"

Add your own ideas:

20 All-Over-The-Place Tips

1) Set up a tournament, playing one of your favorite games. Charades anyone?

2) Host a taffy pull.

3) Bop around town with your friends. Use your phone to make a movie about your birthday.

4) Stop at every restaurant you can and tell them it's your birthday. See how many free desserts you can get.

5) Go to as many movies as you can fit in the day.

6) Ride your favorite rides at an amusement park, over and over.

7) Take a class. The possibilities are endless... art, sculpting, cooking, pottery, knitting, or car repair — anything you want!

8) Go to a deli and get one of everything you like.

9) Take your first musical instrument lesson.

10) Rent a car you've always wanted to drive.

11) Go bowling, mini-golfing, go-cart riding, disc golfing etc.

12) Think of something you've never done, and do it. (Legal and moral of course)

13) Eat cake for breakfast, lunch, and dinner. Have a salad

for dessert.

14) Buy a bunch of toys and take them to a children's hospital. (Get permission)

15) Sleep in. Get up. Eat. Take a nap. Repeat.

16) Find a concert somewhere in the country on your birthday and go.

17) Buy a whole box of your favorite assorted chocolates. Take a bite. Don't like it? Throw it back in the box. This is not to share. It's all about you!

18) Go fishing, snowmobiling, hunting, cliff diving, cross-country skiing…just not all at once.

19) Do something aquatic — take a cruise, a rowboat ride, or go swimming.

20) Throw a fundraiser for your favorite charity. No gifts for you, give them to the charity.

Be careful about this one — only to be used if that's what you really want to do. Don't do it out of guilt or because you think you should. Those thoughts go against all the happy birthday steps!

Add your own ideas:

Use these tips as a brainstorm to spur you on to more ideas of your own. Be you — the happiest birthday version of yourself! Enjoy! Celebrate! Have a Happy Birthday!

But, wait, there's more!

10 Ideas for Celebrations You Can Throw for Yourself! Go for it!

By the way, how do you organize a space party? You planet! (Giggle)

Use these ideas as springboards and catalyst to planning your own out-of-this world party to celebrate YOU!

1) Rent out a planetarium type place and invite all your peeps!

2) Invite everyone to a camping space and have a camp out. Or, do a camp out in your own backyard!

3) Pamper! Whatever that means to you — mani-pedi,

massage, spa day.

4) Organize a competition of crazy events in your own backyard. This could include card tables set up with stations of board games in addition to fun physical feats of strength. There's no limit to what's possible.

5) Put together a scavenger hunt, perhaps one centered on things or places you love.

6) How about those escape rooms, shooting ranges, or places where you throw an axe? (Who could have predicted that would be a thing!)

7) Put together a "roast" where your friends turn into stand-up

comics at your expense. Be ironic — serve roast!

8) Do you live in a colder climate during your birthday or half-birthday? Skating, tubing, skiing, or a sledding party would work. Hot chocolate for all!

9) Pajama party! Everyone wears their (modest, please) PJ's — pop the popcorn, watch movies, and act out your favorite scenes.

10) Craft Day! Everyone brings a craft they enjoy to share and everyone comes away learning something new. How many potholders can you all weave at the party?

See? There are so many ways to have a fun party. Feel weird about having a party for yourself? Go back and read the five steps. You should have the time of your life on your day!

I'd like to leave you with a song.

Happy birthday to you!

Happy birthday to you!

Happy birthday you-smart-person-who-now-knows-how-to-have-a-fun-memorable-fantastic-birthday-every-single- year-now...

Happy birthday to you!

(You sang it, didn't you? Me, too.)

Other books by Michèle Olson

Fiction:

Being Ethel (In a world that loves Lucy)

1979 is getting on Piper Penn's nerves. Struggling to survive past tragedies, she finds comfort in Old Hollywood movies in her native San Francisco. Seeing no reason to adhere to man-made rules after her first-hand look at the ultimate in hypocrisy, Piper does what she wants, and trouble follows.

An unexpected inheritance on a tiny Midwest island in the Straits of Mackinac provides an escape. The mandated stay at the island's glorious Grand Hotel gives her spirits a much-needed boost, especially when she catches the eye of a handsome groundskeeper. Taking part as an extra during the filming of the island movie *Somewhere in Time* adds to her excitement about this turn in her life.

When mysterious accusations and headstrong residents send her into a tailspin, she finds friendship from a quirky, *I Love Lucy* loving nun who challenges her embittered look at life and faith. Can Piper survive the baffling attempts to derail her inheritance before it's too late or has she fallen for a well-planned ruse while falling in love?

"What happens when you combine a love of Lucy, Nora Ephron, Old Hollywood, and the desire for true faith? You embark on an unforgettable 1979 journey to magical, Mackinac Island."

– Author, Michele Olson
Being Ethel (In a world that loves Lucy)

Stay tuned for the release of Book 2 in *A Mackinac Island Story* series.

Being Dorothy
(In a world longing for home)

Meet the Author

Michèle Olson has an over-forty-year career in advertising and marketing as a writer in all mediums. She has also enjoyed a professional voice career including time as a DJ (yes, even when they still played records!) and has voiced local to national commercials and voice projects.

It has always been her dream to segue into being an author with her first fiction project, *Being Ethel (In a world that loves Lucy)*, the first in a series based on Mackinac Island— a tiny island in the Straits of Mackinac that connect the Upper and Lower Peninsula of Michigan. She also loves the world of non-fiction with entertaining "how to" looks at life, including: *5 Easy Steps to a Happy Birthday!*

A mom, a mother-in-love, and a "Gee Gee" (G as in good), Michèle resides with her husband in the shadow of Lambeau Field, where life around football abounds. She cherishes her faith, family, and friends above all, and loves to connect with readers.

Please stay in touch for the latest news from Lake Girl Publishing and sometimes a giveaway!

Facebook.com/LakeGirlPublishing
Twitter @MoDawnWriter
Instagram.com/lakegirlpublishing
My email, (I love to hear from readers!)
Info@LakeGirlPublishing
My website: LakeGirlPublishing.com

My heartfelt thanks and best wishes for your birthday,
          Michèle